Numerology

For

Health and Relationship

Strengthen Relationship,

Enhance Health, Resolve Issues

with Simple Remedies, and Harness

Numerology for Life Balance

DR. ARUN KUMAAR KHANDA

https://arunkumarrk.com

YOUR FREE GIFT

As a token of my gratitude for taking out time to read my book, I would like to offer you a free gift. Click the below link or scan the QR code to download your free eBook PDF

https://arun-kumar-khanda.ck.page/00c46de54c

Acknowledgments

In my journey as an author, I have been blessed with support that has significantly contributed to my success. I am deeply grateful to my mentor and bestselling author, Mr. Som Bathla, for his mentorship, motivation, and guidance in writing, self-publishing, and launching my books, which has been crucial on my path to becoming an author-entrepreneur.

I also extend my heartfelt thanks to my author community, especially to Sooraj Achar, a bestselling author himself, for his timely technical support, encouragement, and invaluable advice, which have made my work much easier.

My gratitude goes out to my readers for their unwavering support. I am also thankful for this incredible platform that provides authors with the resources needed to transform the lives of millions.

Thank you all for being a part of this journey. Readers can connect with me at akkhanda9@gmail.com.

Sincerely,

Arun Kumaar Khanda

TABLE OF CONTENTS

Preface

In today's fast-paced world, we often search for deeper meaning and direction—whether it's in our personal relationships or our journey toward better health. Numerology, an ancient time-tested knowledge offers us a profound way to understand ourselves and the people around us. It is not about superstition but a precise method of aligning our lives with the universal energies that shape our experiences.

This book, ***Numerology for Health and Relationship** *, proves the unique insights that numerology can provide for both your physical well-being and the quality of your relationships. By decoding the secrets hidden in your birth date, we uncover the powerful connection between numbers and life's key aspects—health, love, compatibility, and more. Each number, from Moolanka (birth number) to Bhagyanka (life path number), holds specific energies that can shape your relationships and maintain balance in life.

As you explore the concepts within, you will discover how planetary influences guide your interactions, and how understanding the strengths and challenges of number combinations can empower you to build stronger, more harmonious relationships. Additionally, this book provides easy-to-apply remedies that can help resolve health concerns and restore balance to weak planetary energies, offering a practical roadmap to improve not just your relationships, but your physical and emotional health as well.

Numerology, in its essence, is about self-discovery. It helps you see the unseen, bringing clarity to areas of your life that may have seemed chaotic or confusing. I invite you to take this journey with me, explore the ancient wisdom of numbers, and unlock a healthier, more fulfilling life filled with deeper connections and greater self-awareness.

Life is a journey of growth and understanding, and through numerology, you can open the doors to better health, stronger relationships, and true self-empowerment.

Chapter 1

Introduction to Numerology

What is Numerology?

Numbers have a way of taking a man by the hand and leading him down the path of reason." – Pythagoras

(Pythagoras, the father of numerology, believed that numbers hold the key to understanding the universe.)

Are you interested in learning the concept of numerology? Why is it called numerology? Numerology is the study of numbers. It is a number game. Number speak about your strengths and weaknesses figured in your date of birth. It can speak about your traits, possible profession, health, relationships, education, future trends, etc. It can also provide solutions to your weaknesses.

You are on this page justifies that you are more or less interested in numerology. You may have developed an interest in knowing the secrets of numerology as a knowledge seeker, or need to solve some personal issues with the guidance of numerology or need to put a smile on the faces of thousands.

Before you guide others to follow numerology, you need to be clarified about the core concept of numerology and its basic structure. Am I right? Many questions may appear in your mind about numerology. You may need to get the answers to the following possible questions.

- Is numerology a science or myth?

- Whether numerology has solutions for any issues modern-day people are facing.

- Can numerology predict perfectly?

- Is there any remedies in numerology to rectify the problems?

- Is numerology popular in India or the entire world?

- Is it a proven knowledge?

- How can I benefit from numerology?

- Can it be to improve the standard of living of the people by its applications?

- Is it costly or affordable for a common man?

- Why to believe it?

- Does numerology really work for the upliftment of the birth chart?

- Is numerology a superstition in the eyes of modern science?

- Has it become a game-changer in others' lives?

- Is it a companion of failures or successful people?

So many questions may arise in your mind. Am I right? Four types of people react to numerology differently.

- Some people believe it without questioning and try their luck.

- Second categories believe it after thorough inquiry.

- The third categories believe it is the last refuge after being frustrated running after astrologers, pundits, maulana, etc.

- The fourth category believes numerology is ancient knowledge and wants to acquire it.

You may be one of them. You are the best judge of the situation and circumstances. Remember numerology is an ancient wisdom and knowledge alive for thousands of years. It is near to the belief systems of the millions. If it is not giving any benefits to the people, then why do thousands of numerologists and millions of their clients follow it? You can understand the best as you proceed further. Let us explore the ethics of numbers.

ROLE OF NUMBERS IN YOUR LIFE

Let me tell you the definition of a number. A number is a symbolic representation of an arithmetic value. It is used to count, measure, and label in mathematics. Mathematics is a calculation of numbers and every life is the name of calculated risk. The number is present everywhere, it is omnipresent. It is present here, there and everywhere. It is in your life, his life, the lives of entire creations, the universe.

Nobody can deny the presence of numbers in his life. Can you deny the presence of numbers in your life? You can't deny it. But why?

Hans Decoz says;

"Numbers are the language of the universe, and through numerology, we

can understand the deeper meanings of our lives."

Everything is calculated with numbers. Numbers and you appear to be inseparable when numbers are the language of the universe and you are the product of the universe. You know how numbers follow you for infinite times. Let me remind you of the truth you just forgot.

■ When you are born there are numbers like date and time.

■ When you start your education there is a number like the date of admission, roll number, and class like 1, 2, etc.

■ When you start learning mathematics, you start writing 1,2,3,4, and so on. Because numbers are the foundation of math.

■ When your result is declared you get the mark sheet that contains numbers and percentages.

■ When you get a job, you get a salary, and employee ID again consists of numbers.

■ When you get married on a particular day it is a number.

■ When you open a bank account you get an account number on a particular date.

■ When you ask for a mobile number, you get a ten-digit number (it may vary in different countries).

■ When you buy a motorcycle/car, you get the registration number on the number plate.

■ When you travel on a bus, train, or flight you buy a ticket with a particular number.

■ When you purchase some articles, you pay some currency in numbers.

■ When you live in a house it bears a plot/house number.

■ Your office, factory, farmhouse everything bears an address bearing number.

■ When you are destined to die and leave this physical body it will also be attached with a number.

Now what did you learn from the above exercise? Number is everywhere, and you may not get rid of it. But learn to use the number for your best benefit.

Nine numbers starting from 1 to 9 play very critical roles in deciding the destiny of an individual. Zero is never used in numerology, unlike mathematics. It is also interesting to note that each number is assigned to one planet.

1 is the number that represents the **SUN.**

2 is the number that represents the **MOON.**

3 is the number that represents **JUPITER.**

4 is the number that represents **RAHU**

5 is the number that represents **MERCURY.**

6 is the number that represents **VENUS.**

7 is the number that represents **KETU.**

8 is the number that represents **SATURN.**

9 is the number that represents **MARS.**

In astrology, you can find all the above planets and their effects on the horoscope. But in numerology, we use numbers to predict the future trends. In planet kingdom, some planets are friends with each other and some treat each other as enemies. Some planets behave neutrally as our own society. We behave friendly with some and some act like enemies and few don't care about our cause, the same principles apply to numerology and numbers.

WHY THE DATE OF BIRTH IS IMPORTANT IN NUMEROLOGY?

Have you heard of the term numerology before? Can you imagine only your date of birth can give you a lifetime prediction? Honestly speaking I have not heard of this a few months ago. Do you know your date of birth is special, and the secret is hiding in your date of birth? If you have not treated yourself special to date, you have done injustice to yourself. From now start loving yourself. Treat yourself as special.

You might have faced obstacles and setbacks in your life. You may be disappointed with your fortune. You lost faith in you. You might have visited the astrologers but in vain. Believe me, the secret of your success is hiding in your date of birth. No date of birth is good or bad.

God has given enough to you. Never blame God or Goddess or your parents for your sufferings. Admit you are at fault. You could not find the diamond in the date of birth. Don't worry I will tell you the secret of your date of birth. As a doctor diagnoses the patient, a numerologist analyses the date of birth and prescribes the solution.

It is easy to find the solution for your transformation. It will definitely reduce your struggle. Give a big smile on your face and increase your happiness and well-being.

Numerology very much works for those who implement it in their daily lives.

People and my clients often ask me one question, does numerology really work? The same question I have also asked my mentor. I am now sure that numerology works if applied intelligently. Let you try the concept of numerology in your life and see what magic happens.

Knowledge is everywhere in the books, with our teachers, and on the internet. However, unless you find a way to utilize it for excellence, the same knowledge is of no use to you.

Important Terminology in Numerology

In numerology, you can find terms like Lo-Shu grid, Moolanka(Birth Number), Bhagyanka(Destiny number, Life path number), and Kua number. All the numbers in a date of birth revolve around these terms. There are 81 combinations of MOOLANKA and BHAGYANKA in every date of birth. They indicate your life path and direction. We prepare a Numeroscope or birth chart from your date of birth, where you cannot find the presence of all the 9 numbers, unlike a horoscope. You can find some numbers are present and some are missing from the date of birth.

Lo-Shu Grid:

It is a basic structure upon which the numerological structure stands. One can't think of numerology without a Lo-Shu grid. It is a squire structure containing nine squire structures containing one number. Let me show you the same for a better understanding.

4	9	2
3	5	7
8	1	6

The structure has 3 vertical, 3 horizontal, and 2 diagonal lines. The interesting part of this structure is the sum of all the digits in any line comes to 15. This structure is called the **Laxmi Yantra** in India.

Moolanka:

It is calculated by adding the birth date only. For example, the date of birth of Mr John is 12.4.2012. The birth date is 12. When we add 1 & 2 we get 3(1+2). Now Moolanka of John is 3.

Bhagyanka:

The bhagyanka is calculated by adding the entire date of birth. In this instance case, the Bhagyanka of John comes to (1+2+4+2+1+2=12=1+2=3) 3.

Kua Number:

The calculation of the Kua number is a little bit confusing. In this process, birth year is taken into account. The birth year of John is 2012. If added it comes to 5(2+1+2). Now consider John as male and his Kua number comes to 11-5=6.

Consider a woman born in the year 2012 and her Kua number shall be 4+5=9. Are you interested in knowing why such a calculation? The answer is it is a formula like other mathematical calculations.

Numeroscope;

Date of birth; 12.4.2012

4		222
33		
	11	6

M-3 B-3, K-6

This chart is prepared on the foundation of the Lo-Shu grid. Moolanka, Bhagyanka, and Kua numbers find their proper place in the chart.

Now what do you have observed from the chart? In this chart, four grids are left vacant.

It is observed that out of one million one birth chat, can have all 9 numbers in the chart. It is definitely the rarest of rare events. You can find eight types of lines and eight types of Yogas in the Lo-Shu Grid. From the grid, we find the strengths and weaknesses of the individual. Now you can ask how you can find the hidden treasure from the chart. How can you overcome the weakness of your birth chart?   I have started writing everything in a book series called **Journey Through Numbers.** You can get the answers to your questions from that series. But I can assure you that you will be unstoppable if you can find the secrets to explore your strengths and overcome your weaknesses.

Numerology can explain everything you want to know.

You can find the missing numbers from your date of birth. The missing numbers indicate you are missing something in your life. But nothing to worry about. Every problem has a solution.

"Every problem has a solution, but not necessarily an easy one." – Unknown

Numerology has the solution to the missing numbers.

Name Spelling

Have you ever thought, your name spelling can have positive and negative effects on your career and well-being? Can you imagine your name spelling may foil your plan if not done according to your birth chart? Have you ever heard before that mere name spelling can change your fortune?

Yes, it is a fact. The different case studies suggest that 30-40% of your success or failure depends on your name spelling. If the name spelling is corrected according to your birth date you may get 30-40% more success.

I have corrected my name spelling and getting wonderful results.

Further, we can predict your future years, months, and dates. Future predictions can help you make better decisions for better preparation in your life. When you learn the secrets of success using numerology you can confidently say that the "NUMEROLOGY WORKS 100%". If you want to learn numerology, develop a burning desire to know its perfection. You can read all my books in the series.

WHAT IS THERE FOR YOU IN THIS BOOK?

Are you excited to know what is there in this book for you? This book discusses the characteristics of numbers, anti and opposite combinations, and compatibility of numbers. Nowadays people are struggling to save and enjoy their relationships. This concept has been taken care of.

From time immemorial it has been said that health is wealth. Now health is under serious scrutiny. This book can predict your relationship and its remedies for a better future. It also predicts your marriage whether it will be arranged or love, and predicts your health sectors with remedies.

The beauty of numerology is it only needs a date of birth, no day, time, or place of birth is required, unlike astrology. Do you believe one can choose it as a profession? The answer is **"Yes"** if you complete all the courses sincerely and trained properly. If you give proper attention and work hard as well as smart work you can earn lakhs of rupees per month. If you are in a good profession and happy then no issue, you may use it as your passive income.

You can implement the science of numbers in your life for your perfection. Remember no one is perfect on this planet. Everyone has a scope for improvement. Capacity building and acquiring knowledge give anyone more power. You can use it for the benefit of your family members including your parents, wife/husband, children, friends, and relatives. Imagine you're a small piece of advice that may do wonders in anyone's life. It can put a smile on the lips of many. Then why not implement it? Remember, learning is a continuous process and empowers you more.

Conclusion

Numerology is not just a study of numbers—it's a pathway to understanding the hidden power of life. Your date of birth holds hidden information that needs to be decoded. A properly decoded date of birth can reveal your strengths, weaknesses, and life's direction. By applying the principles of numerology, you can unlock new perspectives on your career, relationships, health, and future. It's not about superstition; it's about harnessing the power of ancient knowledge to improve your life and the lives of those around you.

As we have experienced numbers are everywhere and integral to our existence from birth to death. They are the foundation of the universe, and by understanding their influence, you can do better planning for your personal journey.

Whether you believe in numerology as a science or view it as ancient wisdom its impact is undeniable. Its wise applications in life can make you from weak to strong. As you continue on this path of discovery, remember that numerology offers not just predictions, but practical tools for self-improvement and growth.

Every problem has solutions. Never be disappointed in your life. Life is not a bed of roses but of challenges. Face the challenges with the solutions of numerology and unlock your true potential.

Chapter 2

Number Game: The Characteristics of Numbers

**"The universe cannot be read until we have learned the language and become familiar with the characters in which it is written. It is written in mathematical language, and the letters are triangles, circles, and other geometrical figures, without which means it is humanly impossible to comprehend a single word."
– Galileo Galilei**

Everyone bears a specific character and trait, which makes them unique and separates them from the crowd. Everyone is unique in the creation. However, very few attract the attention of others. Why? It is their characteristics that make them identified as such.

For example, when we talk about a person, we may say "he is good and intelligent but proud. He often demands respect but doesn't command it. However, he is a good soul, helps the poor whenever he is approached," etc.

"Rosy is a beautiful girl but not worthy of being respected".

Now what do you understand from the above two examples? These are the qualities of the persons, both positive and negative called their characteristics. As every human being bears some qualities good and bad, every number also bears some bad and good qualities. As you know every number from 1 to 9 represents nine planets, the presence of the numbers in the birth chart exhibits those characters of the planets.

Let us begin now. REMEMBER WHEN WE TALK ABOUT THE CHARACTERISTICS OF NUMBERS, IT IS ABOUT THE CHARACTERISTICS OF THE **MOOLANKA** OF A NUMEROSCOPE NOTHING MORE.

1∎

Number one represents the sun, the king of the numbers. Can you calculate how we find number 1 from a date of birth? Can you guess it? Yes, you are right. It comes from, 1, 10,19, & 28. (1+0=1, 1+9=10=1,2+8=10=1). Although the sum of all the numbers is the same, they can have exhibited a little bit different characteristic.

CHARACTERISTICS

Number 1 is the number of the sun. The people with Moolanka 1 can have the following characteristics;

- They are born leaders. They often rise to the highest rank and file even if started small. They may be the leader of a team, pressure group, organization, etc. Politics may suit them. But don't like petty politics.

- They are high-minded. They can find their own path, for which they are the pioneer. They are hardworking people.

- They are authoritative and command respect for their work and activities.

- They are boss. Administrations suit them much. They are perfectionist and dominating. They don't allow other people to rule over them.

- They are resilient people. They believe setbacks are temporary and stepping stones for success. Never accept defeat as a permanent feature.

- They can become good politician, and leaders and do good in government departments.

- They can become good entrepreneurs and trendsetters.

- They are faithful and royal like lions.

- They are egoistic, rigid, and stubborn at some point in time.

- They are prestige conscious and asking for help for their own purpose is difficult.

Overall, people with Moolanka 1 are royal, pioneer, hardworking, leader, and authoritative. They believe in perfection and themselves.

All the above features can be seen in 1, 10, 19, and 28. But in the case of 19, they are more successful than other numbers.

2∎

Number 2 represents the moon, given the status of queen. 2 represents water and motherhood. How can you get the number 2 from the date of birth? It can be 2, 11, 20, and 29.

CHARACTERISTICS

You have seen the moon. How pleasant and beautiful is it? But it grows in the bright fortnight or WAXING PHASE of the moon (Shukla Paksha) for 15 days and diminishes in the dark fortnight or WANING PHASE of the moon (Krishna Paksha) for 15 days. It justifies that the people of Moolanka 2 are not stable in mind. They may not be the consistent performer. Their performances may not be up to mark on some occasions. They sometimes behave like an immature child.

We can say, they are;

- On some occasions they are indecisive in their actions and behave like immature chap.

- They are good-looking, soft-hearted, and attractive.

- They are good planner but at the same time very lazy.

- They always compromise things when things turn ugly in relationships.

- They are blessed with sensitivity, kindness, and harmony but these people often suffer from mood swings.

- **There is every apprehension for them to go into depression, making their lives difficult.**

- They are very cooperative and supportive. They also need support for their growth.

- They are feminine characters. They love and feel comfortable in the company of females.

- They are good healer, social workers, and counselors.

- They are diplomats and mediators.

- They love a peaceful environment.

- They can work for the best customer satisfaction.

In conclusion, I can say Moolanka 2, are good soul. They are soft-spoken, gentle, diplomat, and look attractive. They need support and provide support.

However, there is a twist to the number 29. The people born on the 29th of any month may witness marriage issues. If married without a matching birth chart may face difficulties in married life. However, it is not a universal conclusion. It depends on other numbers also in the chart.

3.

Number 3, is Jupiter, the Guru of gods. He is

pious in his approach and attitude. Let us see how can we find 3. It can be 3, 12, 21, and 30.

CHARACTERISTICS

Let us see the characteristics of number 3.

- ✓ People of Moolanka 3 are driven by knowledge. They always need to be knowledgeable and hungry for it. **Sometimes they prefer knowledge to money.**

- ✓ They are creative people and innovative in their thought processes.

- ✓ They are problem solvers and optimistic people.

- ✓ THEY THINK OUTSIDE THE BOX and have a unique approach to day-to-day life issues.

- ✓ They can imagine and visualize things better.

- ✓ They may be good at art, literature and music.

- ✓ The teaching profession may suit them better.

- ✓ **They can also do well in administration, police, bank, politics, salesmen, and technology.**

- ✓ They are spiritual at their heart.

- ✓ They may be religious in practice in daily life.

- ✓ They love mystic science and occult.

- ✓ They focus on accomplishment and success.

- ✓ They are good communicators and very good at public speaking.

In conclusion, I can suggest that **the people ruled by Moolanka 3, should never touch liquor and eat non-vegetarian food.**

Overall, these people are the **powerhouse of knowledge and good soul**. You can ask them for advice to solve any issues relating to personal importance. They can be educated, religious, and spiritually minded. Occult professions can be best suited to them.

4∙

Number 4 represents Rahu. We can call him

Robinhood in numerology. We can get 4 from the date of birth of 4, 13, 22 and 31.

13 IS A KARMIC NUMBER AND IS TREATED AS INAUSPICIOUS.

But why? Because it is believed that it has a debt and sin of the previous incarnations.

In Europe and many Western countries, there is no lane no 13. In many cities houses or flats, no 13 are not given due to this belief of karmic number.

At the end of MYAN CALENDER's 13th Bakun was superstitiously feared as a harbinger of the apocalyptic 2012 phenomenon. The fear of number 13 has a specifically recognized phobia, triskaidekaphobia, a word first recorded in 1911.

Further, 4 is associated with death for Cantonese-speaking Chinese people.

CHARACTERISTICS

- ✓ The people having Moolanka 4 are rowdy and rebellious. They need to follow their own rules and independent character.

- ✓ They are energetic, knowledgeable, clever, and confident.

- ✓ **They are born with leadership qualities and diligence.**

- ✓ They love discipline, act in it, and want others to follow it.

- ✓ They are logical people. They believe in logic and remain in search of logic in everything. They can't believe anything without logic.

- ✓ They are confidential and secretive. You may believe them undoubtedly.

- ✓ They are short-tempered and argumentative. They get angry for simple things.

- ✓ **They are also abusive and use vulgar language to anyone.**

- ✓ They are impulsive and sometimes encouraging and motivating.

- ✓ They are good planners.

- ✓ Best-suited career for them in *project management, accounting, engineering, and organizing units.*

People with Moolanka 4 are disciplined, rebellious, secretive, logical, impulsive, and simultaneously abusive. IN MANDARIN, THE NUMBER 4 IS PRONOUNCED AS "SI", WHICH SOUNDS SIMILAR TO THE WORD DEATH. It is due to superstition connected with the number 4.

5■

Number 5, is the number of Mercury, the prince. In the Lo-Shu grid, you can find it positioned at the center of all the numbers. It gives balance to the life. We can find the number 5 from the date of birth of 5, 14, and 23.

CHARACTERISTICS

- ✓ People with 5 as a Moolanka enjoy a very peaceful and balanced life. They know how to balance ***and manage finance, life, and relationships.***

- ✓ They take responsibility for their own life and are accountable for up and downs of their lives. They never like outside interference in their lives.

- ✓ They are lazy people and never prefer physical labor and exercise. They may be fat due to good eating habits and lack of physical exercise. However, many things depend on the Bhagyanka also.

- ✓ They are romantic people and love their partner much. They are young at heart and self-loving. They are very careful about themselves.

- ✓ They are successful people. They can excel in their professional and personal life.

- ✓ **They can be good writers and can excel in marketing and travel agencies.**

- ✓ They can be good entrepreneurs.

- ✓ The people with 5 Moolanka are lucky because they have no non-friends or enemies.

- ✓ They are resilient people and often bounce back smartly.

- ✓ They are talkative and sometimes become chatterboxes.

- ✓ They are independent and desire to find fresh solutions to problems.

- ✓ They are social and find connections with others. However, their impatience can sometimes lead to conflicts.

✓ They are good communicators and adapt
    to any situation.

Overall, people of number 5 are romantic, self-cared, accountable, and blessed. They are born to success.

6.

Let us talk about Venus, the number 6. You know Venus as the councilor of demons. We can get 6 from the date of birth 6, 15, and 24.

CHARACTERISTICS

The people having 6 as their Moolanka exhibit the following characteristics.

✓ They are romantic people. They love to enjoy life. **Prefer to live in luxury and glamor.**

✓ They are manipulative. Often resort to lying. But they present the lie as a fact. You can't detect them lying.

✓ They are diplomatic and intelligent. Manage things properly and responsibly.

✓ They love sex and like to tour and travel.

- ✓ They are also family men, love their children much, and are cared for by their children.

- ✓ They are trustworthy, sympathetic, and gentle.

- ✓ Professions like hospitality(hotel), teaching, and health care, nursing(doctors) can suit them.

- ✓ They can do well in social service.

- ✓ They can excel in music and acting professions.

- ✓ **They should not marry Moolanka numbers 2,3, and 9.**

In conclusion, I may say they are loving, romantic, and manipulative. Manage things diplomatically. They are family men.

However, there is an apprehension of marriage-related issues in the case of females, if 6 is coming from 24. It is observed that in such a case female creates the issues. But nothing to worry about, every problem has a solution.

7.

Who is 7? Guess it. You are right it is Ketu the headless thinker planet. We can get the number from 7, 16, & 25.

CHARACTERISTICS

The people with the number 7 as Moolanka may have the following characteristics.

- ✓ They are the people of Golden Heart. They think from the heart not from the head, as Ketu is headless.

- ✓ They are very simple and believe everything is truth without thinking of its logical conclusion.

- ✓ **They are highly educated and do research in different fields**.

- ✓ They are betrayed in love due to their simplicity.

- ✓ They are spiritual people of the religious band of minds.

- ✓ Occult profession is most suited to them. They can earn name, fame, and money if chosen as a profession.

- ✓ They may be good in education if opted for a career.

- ✓ **Health, research, philosophy, and, psychology, sectors may suit them.**

- ✓ Marriage life may not be so smooth.

- ✓ They are the people of wisdom.

Number 7 is a symbol of disappointment. The people may be disappointed in love life, money, health, and marriage. But they are highly educated, men of wisdom and kind-hearted.

8.

Let us see number 8, Saturn, the lord of karma and justice. We can get the number 8 from the date of birth; 8,17, & 26.

CHARACTERISTICS

You know that number 8, is a number of struggles. Saturn is a slow planet. The people born with 8 as the Moolanka are normally struggling in life. If you talk about the order of struggles, I may say the struggle can increase from 17,8, and 26 respectively. In fact, the struggle is the benchmark for this number and nothing can be owned easily without effort. The characteristics of 8 may include;

- ✓ They are likely to struggle in life. May not get anything easily.

- ✓ Everything gets delayed in their lives. The work that is supposed to be completed today can be completed tomorrow.

- ✓ **They are hardworking and industrious. They are resilient and can achieve anything.**

- ✓ They are task-oriented and committed. Unless the task is complete, they never relax.

- ✓ **They are good orator and good at heart. They look like task master but at the same time very understanding.**

- ✓ They believe in their efforts and qualities of work. It is very difficult to convince them.

- ✓ They are slow but down-to-earth people. Understands others very well.

- ✓ The law sector is the most suited profession for them.

- ✓ **They are born to lead and the money market can suit them best. CEO and high-powered executives are best for them.**

✓ THEY THINK THEY ARE THE BEST AND MOST AMBITIOUS.

✓ They are super disciplined with a smile on their face.

✓ They are natural leaders and sources of inspiration for others.

✓ **They love money**(legal) and may forget the most important things like friendships and relaxation for it.

It is observed that women with 8 as a Moolanka may struggle in their marriage life. They may not get a suitable life partner or if married conjugal life mayn't be so successful. They may face problems during pregnancy.

9.

Now we are at last number 9. Nine represents the planet Mars. Mars is a warrior, a commander. We can get 9, from the date of birth; 9, 18, 27.

CHARACTERISTICS

- They are MOOD-DRIVEN PEOPLE and never compromise with their principles.

- They are egoistic people and prefer death to loss/compromise.

- They are disciplined. They can be most suited to the ARMY, AND POLICE.

- They are **unpredictable characters.**

- **They are spiritual leaders, compassionate and humanitarian pursuits.**

- They believe in idealism and desire to make a meaningful difference in the world.

- They are DONOR LIKE THE MYTHICAL HERO KARNA.

- Son and father relations very deteriorating.

  IF A MALE HAS A DATE OF BIRTH OF 18, YOU CAN BLINDLY SAY FATHER-SON RELATIONSHIPS ARE AT A LOW LEVEL. The son doesn't want to see the face of his father. You may be shocked by these predictions, but there are solutions. If the son is in the study, put him in the hostel. Never do business jointly. Avoid staying together under the same roof.

- They may have lost their father before they were born or during childhood.

People of Moolanka 9 are disciplined, mood-driven, egoistic, compassionate, humanitarian, and unpredictable character.

Anti and Opposite Combinations

I have told you earlier that some planets behave as enemies to each other and some find themselves as friends. Some bear opposite characters but are not enemies to each other. In the case of the opposite planets, we can do remedies for their upliftment in the birth chart. However, it is not possible in the case of anti-planets. Here I am talking about the combination of Moolanka and Bhagyanka. Let me tell you which are the anti and the opposite planets in numerology. Now see the table below.

Anti-M-B

M	B
1	8
2	8
8	2
3	6
6	3
8	1

Opposite M-B

M	B
4	2
2	4
4	9
9	4
9	9
7	7

Combinations of 1 & 8 or,8 &1

One is the Sun and 8 is Saturn. In Indian Mythology, they are father and son. But why are they enemies of each other?

Let me tell you the story behind it. Once the Sun god was attracted toward Chhaya and from their love life a son was born to the couple. Later the son was named Saturn. Saturn was so dark in complex, that the sun refused to recognize him as his son in public. Rather offered him wealth, property, money, etc. but Saturn refused to accept anything but recognition which was not possible on the part of the sun god. The sun even did not recognize Chhaya as his wife, which made Saturn furious. From that day Saturn never respect his father Sun, rather remain in readiness to hurt him. A compromise between the two is impossible, which made both the planets anti.

Combinations of 2 & 8 or, 8 & 2:

2 is the moon and 8 is Saturn. One is milky white and the other is dark in complex. One is feminine character and the other is masculine. One is water and the other is iron. What would happen if the iron came in contact with water? The answer is known to you. Iron will get rusted.

Mythology says the sun denied Chhaya as his wife due to the moon his beautiful queen. This attitude of the sun infuriated Saturn. From that day Saturn treats the moon as his enemy like the sun.

Combination of 3 & 6 or 6 & 3:

3 and 6 both are the powerhouse of knowledge. But they can't tolerate each other. Do you know why? Because, both 3 and 6 represent two different ideologies, two different mindsets, and two different civilizations. 3 is guru Brihaspati or Jupiter is the principal advisor of the devas or Gods. On the other hand, 6, Venus the Guru of Danavas or demons. Both Devas and Danavas fight each other for supremacy and better living. Both the masters represent different civilizations and ideologies, and they never compromise their community's interest making them enemies.

Combinations of 4 & 2 or 2 & 4:

This is a combination of opposite numbers. In this combination 4 is Rahu a Rabinhood-like character, and 2 is queen. Queen never like the company of Rahu but 4 has no problem with 2 but 2 has.

As written (in Puranas) mythology both Devas and Danavas churn the milk ocean. All the precious items and elements that evolved from the ocean were distributed among the gods and Rishis. Finally, the **nectar** of immortality known as ***"Amrit"*** was found. Both decided to eat it but there was an apprehension of being misused by demons. That is why Vishnu in the guise of beautiful enchantress Mohini, offered to distribute it to both. Danavas being mesmerized by the beauty of Mohini agreed to the proposal.

However, Rahu in the guise of God consumed the nectar, and it made the sun and moon aware. They immediately intimate the matter to Vishnu. Vishnu to establish divine order asked Sudarshan chakra/disk to cut the head of Rahu. As Rahu consumed nectar, he did not die but lived with two parts. Rahu is the upper part as head and Ketu is its lower part as a body.

Rahu from that moment had a grudge against the sun and moon, as a result, it is believed that Rahu periodically shallow the Sun and moon causing an eclipse. As Rahu has no body the sun and moon escape his grasp.

Rahu reflects the illusion, deception, and darker aspects of life.

On the other hand, the Moon reflects mind, emotion, and inner self. Both 2 & 4 represent different characters branding them opposite numbers.

Combinations of 4 & 9 or 9 & 4:

Rahu (4) and Mars(9) are opposite to each other. Why opposite? Because both are opposite characters. Rahu is a gangster and Mars is a commander. King is nearer to Mars. Rahu needs freedom but Mars does not allow him to be free. Mars is a pious sanyasi but Rahu is a demon who bears negative sentiments.

Combinations of 9 & 9:

Mars and Mars combinations are opposite as both are ego-driven and unpredictable.

Combinations of 7 & 7:

7 is Ketu the lower part of the body. It is a number of struggles. 7 represents wisdom but without knowledge wisdom is meaningless. Hence, they are placed in opposite categories.

Conclusion:

In numerology, each number holds its own unique characteristics, much like individuals possess distinct traits. Starting from numbers 1 to 9 aligned with planets shaping personality, behavior, and life outcomes. For instance, the leadership and resilience of Moolanka 1 reflect the influence of the Sun, while the emotional sensitivity and diplomacy of Moolanka 2 mirror the qualities of the Moon.

As we move through the numbers, we see different attributes emerge—Jupiter's wisdom in Moolanka 3, Rahu's rebellious nature in Moolanka 4, Mercury's balance in Moolanka 5, and so on. Each number brings both strengths and challenges, reminding us that every individual is a blend of qualities, much like the numbers themselves.

The fascinating part of numerology is understanding the characteristics of anti and opposite numbers. For example, the friction between Moolanka 1 and 8 reflects the ancient story of the Sun and Saturn, where the differences are deeply rooted yet irreconcilable.

Ultimately, numerology provides a powerful tool to comprehend human nature, and at the same time offers insight into our strengths, weaknesses, and potential paths. It guides us to understand ourselves better and the world around us.

Now you understand the characteristics of the numbers. In the next chapter, we see how the numbers (Moolanka & Bhagyanka) behave with each other.

Now this much for this chapter. I hope you understand it well and can use it for the purpose most suited for you. You may be excited to know its veracity of characteristics. It is a good sign that you are interested in numerology. Collect some dates of birth of your friends and relatives and find out the secrets hiding behind them.

Chapter 3

Compatibility of Numbers

Everything in the universe has a rhythm, everything dances." – Maya Angelou

(In numerology, the vibration of numbers is often seen as part of the rhythm that governs life.)

Compatibility means the rhythm of frequencies. If the frequencies are matched, they are friends, on the other hand, they are non-friends. Every number has some friends, non-friends, and neutral numbers. You can say the neutral number as mute spectators. Let me draw a table for better appreciation.

No	Friends	Non-Friends	Neutral
1	9,2,5,3,6,1	8	4,7
2	1,5,3,2	8,4,9	6,7

3	1,5,3,2,7*	6	4,8,9,7*
4	7,1,5,6,4*,8*	4*,8*,2,9	3
5	1,2,3,6,5	....	7,8,9,4
6	1,5,7,6	3	8,9,2,4
7	4,6,1,3,5	....	2,8,9,7
8	5,6,3,7,4*,8*	(4*,8*,)1,2,	9
9	1,5,3	4,2	6,7,8,9

Let me explain the above chart in detail.

1.

1 represents the sun, the king of the planetary system. The sequence of friends is as follows 9,2,5,3,6,1. You can say it is the king's number. It is royal in its approach, attitude, and attire. He runs an empire. What does a king need to run a kingdom, an empire? Expand the empire? Annex and conquer the kingdom of the enemy? Can you guess? It is obviously an army or military power. Who is the commander of the military? The answer is no 9, Mars. That is why 1 king is very close to Commander 9. 9 is the best friend of 1. The king can only share some secrets with the

commander. It can't even be shared with his beloved wife (queen).

Our history witnesses the mutiny of the commanders against kings and the seizure of power by army commanders. Now it is clear that the king is nearest to 9.

After number 9, next nearer to number 1 is number 2, the queen. If you want peace in family and pleasure in conjugal life, you must love, care, and respect your wife, otherwise, your life will be no less than a hell. King is not an exception to it.

Then comes 5, the prince, the future king. King needs his support to run the empire whenever needed. Further, 5 needs to learn the art of administration from his father. Next come 3, 6 the councilors, and 1(king) in decreasing orders of priority as shown in the table.

You may ask how 1 is a friend of 1. One answer is self-love, and another answer is a king needs to keep good relations with his counterparts in the neighboring states for peace and prosperity in the region.

Now let's talk about the non-friend column. Here 8, Saturn is the lonely enemy of 1, the Sun. Why Saturn is the enemy of the Sun?

The sun is a symbol of light and heat energy. The heat can melt the iron at 1,538°C or 2,800°F. Iron is an element of Saturn. In the presence of heat, iron can't establish its regular shape. This is why both heat and iron can't stay together. Further coal is also associated with Saturn. Heat can ignite coal easily. From the scientific point of view heat iron, and coal can't coexist together.

Further, there is a myth found in many Puranas, about the relationships of the Sun and Saturn. According to the myth, Saturn is the illegitimate child of the Sun, born to mother Chaya. Sun entered into a relationship with Chaya but did not get her married or recognize her as his wife. The son born to their relationship, Saturn was very dark in complex, for which the sun did not acknowledge him as his son. Saturn demands his recognition as the son of the sun, but the sun refuses it, rather than offering a palace, money, property, etc. As the matter was not settled amicably, Saturn maintained his enmity with his father the sun forever.

In a neutral column, you can find 4 and 7. One is gangster and another is headless. A king doesn't need their support and at the same time may not apply his forces against them.

2.

Number 2 is the moon, called queen. In the friends list you can see the following sequence. 1,5,3,2. What you have noticed? Who comes first as a friend of the queen? It is king, her beloved husband. Can a CHEST WIFE live without her husband? The answer is known to you.

After the king, the queen needs her son, the prince of the empire, the future king. Then comes 3, the councilor. In the time of crisis, his advice can save the kingdom. Next comes 2, the queen and her counterparts.

Now see her non-friend's column. Who are they? 8,4,9. First comes 8, Saturn the stepson. A friendly relationship between a stepmother and a stepson may not normally exist.

If we see it from a scientific point of view, the moon represents water, and Saturn represents iron. The combination of iron and water makes the iron rust. It is better for them to keep their distance. That is why both 2 and 8 can't stay together in a single column.

4 is gangster. Queen doesn't like gangsters. As a woman, one should not like such an unworthy fellow. Next comes number 9, the commander. Queen hates the commander because the king spends most of his time consulting with 9. Further, 9 does not take command from the queen except the king.

Next, come the neutral planets of the moon. Numbers 6 and 7 are neutral to number 2. Because the queen rarely needs the advice of Venus, the guru of devils, or demons. Jupiter is always available to guide the queen as and when necessary. Ketu (7) is headless, how can he support the queen? Number 2 has no enmity or friendship with Ketu. He is left as neutral.

3.

Number 3 is Jupiter, the guru of gods. He is powerhouse of knowledge, pious and vegetarian. His friends come in the following sequence i.e. 1,5,3,2,7*. He is most friendly with the king. Next comes 5, the prince as his friend. The next friend of Jupiter is Jupiter himself. Here both are councilors and respect each other. Number 3 has no problem with 2 or queen. Jupiter is the symbol of knowledge. 7 is the symbol of wisdom. Knowledge and wisdom have a positive equation making them friends.

Number 6 is positioned as a non-friend of number 3. You may ask why. Both 3 and 6 are councilors, both are powerhouses of knowledge. Then why they are non-friends? Because there is a basic difference between the two. 3 is the councilor of gods/devata and 6 is the councilor of demons/danav (Asuras). Both are from different ideologies, as gods and demons are enemies to each other.

Further, 4,8,9,7 are neutral for Jupiter. Because number 3, has no business with 4,8,9,7 (7 may become his friend sometimes due to his wisdom).

4.

Number 4 is Rahu. Can you tell me who would be his best friend? I think you guessed it correctly. It is number 7, Ketu, the lower part of Rahu. The combination of 4 and 7 not only completes the body but also completes the thinking pattern. 4 is a good gangster he needs the support of the king to remain in freedom. That is why made friends with 5, the future king. Next comes 6, in his friend list, because both share a common *tamasic character*.

2 and 9 are non-friends of 4. Because the queen doesn't need the support of a gangster or believe in him, the characteristics of 9 and 4 are completely different.

Now 4 & 8, both may be friends if their relationship is not permanent. Both may be non-friends if their relationships are made permanent.

You are now a little bit confused by the above statement. Am I right? Let me explain if the people of 4 Moolanka make friends, then it is okay. But if the simple friendship turns into a permanent relationship in the form of marriage, or business partner it can't survive.

You find only Jupiter in the neutral column. Gangsters may seek the advice of Jupiter but number 3 keeps a safe distance from it.

5.

Number 5 is Mercury, the prince.

The sequence of friends comes as follows 1,2,3,6,5.

The prince is closer to his father, the king, then his mother comes second. He has a good rapport with both the councillors 3 and 6. A prince has a good friendship with another prince. Hence 5 is a friend of 5.

It is important to note that a prince has no non-friend. Because when you see the Lo-Shu Grid you can find that 5 is positioned at the center, keeping an equal distance from all the blocks. As a prince 5, maintain neutrality with **7,8,9,4**. Similarly, 7,8,9,4 have no problem with the future king 5.

6.

Number 6 is Venus, the guru of demons, better known as ***Sukracharya***. He believes in empowerment and the upliftment of demons. As a councilor, he is close to the king. Next in closeness come 5, the prince. Number 7, (Ketu) is also his friend because 7 is the disciple of 6. Further, number 6 is the friend of 6, a councilor can be a friend of a councilor.

6 has one non-friend in 3. Because 6 is the guru of demons and 3 is the guru of gods. ***Both can't see each other, as both are anti-planet.*** Next, come the neutral numbers in the form of 8,9,2,4. Number 6 has no problem with them.

7.

Number 7 is Ketu. I have told you earlier that Ketu is a shadow planet and the myth behind it. It has no head. Now can you guess who would be his best friend? I feel your presumption is right. It is Rahu, number 4. When 7 is associated with 4 a complete body is formed, as they are made for each other. The next close friend of Ketu is Venus, number 6. Venus is the mentor of 7. They have a relationship of a teacher and a disciple.

Next comes number 1, the king. Being headless he thinks from heart for which he needs the blessings of the king. Jupiter 3, is coming in the queue as the next friend, as Jupiter represents knowledge and 7 represents wisdom. Knowledge is always comfortable with wisdom. Next comes number 5, the prince as the friend of Ketu.

Ketu has no non-friends like Prince Mercury. Now let us see who are the neutral planets for Ketu. They are 8,2,9,7. It is understood that 8, 2, and 9 are neutral for 7, but how and why 7 is neutral for 7? The reason is obvious as 7 is headless and it thinks from the heart. Its thinking is illogical then how an illogical thinker can help another illogical thinker? So, it is better to say 7 is neutral to 7 rather than calling them friends.

8.

Now talk about number 8, Saturn. He administers justice for all. He is a judge and never does injustice to anyone. Have you ever seen the justices of a high court or supreme court? How they maintain neutrality, without much involvement in social gatherings and functions.

Planet Mercury, number 5, is his friend. Number 5 is a prince and a small boy, who may not have any work with a judge, which is why 8 has a friend in his step-brother 5. Other friends of 8 are 6,3,7. Numbers 3 and 6 are persons of knowledge as they are councilors to the king. The judge needs their advice for the administration of justice. Ketu thinks from the heart and may not do any mischief, so he is the friend of 8.

Now see these numbers 4*,8*. Relation of 4 and 8 with 8 is friendly when they are occasionally getting together. They are fine in temporary relationships simply as friends. But they may be non-friends if the temporary relationship is further promoted to permanent relationships like marriage, or business partnerships (between 4 & 8, 8 & 8). In simple language, **I CAN SAY THAT PERMANENT RELATIONSHIPS CAN'T SURVIVE BETWEEN 8 & 8, 8 & 4, AND 4 & 4.**

Now you can anticipate who are the enemy or non-friends of Saturn. The number one enemy is the sun, and the second is number 2. Saturn is the illegitimate child of the sun and the sun can't recognize number 8 as his son, for which he always sees the opportunity to take revenge. Moon is the queen and his stepmother. He considers that due to the beauty of his stepmother, his mother is not recognized as a queen of the sun. Furthermore, if we look from a scientific point of view, the moon is water and Saturn is iron. If both the elements come together iron gets rust. Hence, they are antiplanets, better for them to keep away from each other.

The red planet Mars, number 9 is the neutral number for 8.

9.

Number 9 is Mars, the commander. He is unpredictable and a fighter planet. Often driven by mood. His friends include 1,5,3. Being given command in the army he is obliged to king. Next comes 5, the prince, the future king. Number 3, Jupiter is the friend of number 9, because he needs advice from the guru.

4 and 2 are non-friends of 9. Rahu is a gangster who can't patch up with the commander. No doubt 2 is queen but 9 doesn't carry out her order. There is a mental war that always runs between the two. **More both 4 and 8 are struggling planets. When comes together make the people struggle, struggle, and struggle.**

6,7,8,9 are neutral planets for number 9. How 9 can be neutral for 9. When a commander meets another commander maintain constraint and avoid confrontation. It is the part of discipline that 9, follows, for which 9 is neutral to nine.

Now this is much toward compatibility of numbers. We will know more further in the subsequent chapters.

Conclusion:

In this chapter, the compatibility of numbers, we see how each number vibrates at its own frequency, creating relationships that mirror real-life dynamics. The concept of compatibility is beautifully illustrated through the lens of friendship, neutrality, and enmity, with each number representing a celestial or mythological entity. For example, the Sun (1) and Saturn (8) clash like fire and iron, while the Sun's strong bond with Mars (9) signifies the unbreakable connection between a king and his commander. These patterns give us insight into how numbers influence our relationships, both personal and professional.

Ultimately, understanding the compatibility of numbers allows us to understand better our interactions and make informed decisions. Whether building friendships, partnerships, or alliances, knowing the rhythm of these numbers can guide us toward harmonious outcomes or help us avoid potential conflicts.

As we continue, and learn more about this fascinating subject, we'll uncover deeper layers of meaning and practical applications that help align our lives with the cosmic rhythm around us.

Prediction of Your Relationship from Your Birth Chart with Remedies.

Numerology is the bridge between who you are and who you have the potential to be. – Anonymous

(A common view in numerology is that numbers reveal deeper insights into personal growth.)

Man is a social animal for his social connection. However, just social connection is not enough to maintain a healthy family and social life. For this purpose, he needs a strong emotional bond. A viable and strong relationship depends on many factors, like social background, upbringing, education, and environment. For example, you can't expect good and polished behavior from an uncultured man.

However, in numerology combinations of some numbers, the combination of Moolanka and

Bhagyanka is responsible for favorable, unfavorable, or broken relationships. We can clearly detect it from your relationships, from your birth chart.

Number 6:

Number 6 is very crucial in any form of relationship. 6 is the symbol of luxury & glamor, enjoyment, relationships, merrymaking, etc. It represents care, home, love, and family. They are gentle, loving, and caregivers. **In astrology and numerology, Venus is a key player in marriage and married life.**

Presence of 77 or more in the birth chart:

If number 6 is absent and 77 or more 7 are present, it is presumed that the married life of the person is in bad shape. He or she may be involved in pre-marital or post-marital relationships. There is also a possibility of multiple affairs and illicit relationships.

Combination of Moolanka & Bhagyanka:

Next comes the combination of numbers (Moolanka & Bhagyanka) of your birth chart. If **number 6 is absent** and the following Moolanka and Bhagyanka combination is present, it can be concluded that the relationship sector is weak.

M	B
1	8

8	1
2	8
8	2
3	6
6	3
7	7
2	9
4	4
6	9
4	8
8	8
9	9

Why the above combinations are not preferred in relationships?

I have explained it earlier, however, once again let me explain the fact.

Numbers 1 & 8:

Number 1 is the Sun and number 8 is Saturn. As per Vastu the Sun is the lord of the east and Saturn is the lord of the west. The sun represents vitality and power with gold, red, and orange colors. On the other hand, Saturn represents black.

The sun is light and heat, whereas Saturn is coal and iron. Numbers 1 and 8 exhibit opposite directions and characters. Further, heat can melt the iron and change its shape. Hence their relationship is under stress. As per mythology both 1 and 8 are father & son in a relationship but non friend to each other. They are considered anti-planets in numerology.

FURTHER MARRIAGE BETWEEN TWO PEOPLE WITH MULANKA -BHAGYANKA 1 & 8 CAN'T SURVIVE. IT IS WISE TO AVOID THIS RELATIONSHIP.

Remedies:

Uplift the numbers 5, & 6. Mercury and Venus are the common friends of 1 & 8.

Numbers 2 and 8:

The moon is number 2. Its colors are white, silver, and light blue. The moon represents water. Saturn represents iron. If iron comes in contact with water, it rusts. It is a myth the moon is the queen of the king the Sun. The beauty of the moon attracted the sun leading to the decline of Chaya (mother of Saturn) as his queen making Saturn angry with the moon. Under these circumstances, any form of relationship for such a person is not viable.

MOREOVER, A PERMANENT RELATIONSHIP LIKE A MARRIAGE BETWEEN TWO PEOPLE WITH 2-8 AS MOOLANKA OR BHAGYANKA MAY NOT SURVIVE.

Remedies:

Uplift 5, & 3, in the birth chart as both are friends of 2 & 8.

Number 3 & 6:

Numbers 3 & 6 represent the planets Jupiter and Venus respectively. Both are the powerhouse of knowledge. But they represent different ideologies and lifestyles. Jupiter is the guru of devas or gods, whereas Venus is the guru and idealogue of asura or demons. They are antiplanets. A person with 3&6 as Moolanka & Bhagyanka mayn't enjoy good relationships.

WHENEVER WE TALK ABOUT A MARRIAGE RELATIONSHIP, MARRIAGE BETWEEN 3 & 6 (MOOLANKA OR BHAGYANKA) MAY NOT SURVIVE TO ITS FULL POTENTIAL. SUCH A MARRIAGE PROPOSAL MUST BE AVOIDED.

Remedies:

Uplift 1,5, & 7, numbers in the birth chart, as the sun, mercury, and Ketu are the friends of 3 & 6.

Number 7 & 7:

Number 7 represents Ketu, the headless planet. It can think from the heart but can't think from its brain. If you have both Moolanka and Bhagyanka are 7, then you may have multiple affairs. Your family life may come under severe storms and scrutiny. Further, people with multiple 7 in their birth chart are attracted to love marriage. If the chart is supported by the presence of 6 then the marriage can sustain.

Remedies:

Uplift the following numbers in a birth chart. 4,6,1,5.

Number 2 & 9:

In the case of marriage and relationship, Moolanka 2 and Bhagyanka 9 and vice-versa

are not considered stable. Moon (2) is a queen and 9 is a commander. 2 is beautiful and 9 does not like sex or the company of women. 9 is saint-like and doesn't believe in romance which 2 likes.

Remedies:

Uplift the following numbers 1,5,3 in the birth chart.

Number 6 & 9:

Six is Venus and 9 is Mars. If 6 Moolanka & 9 Bhagyanka and vice-versa, get married, that may not be stable. 6 believe in love, family, and romance but 9 is a saint like. The character of both numbers may mismatch, leading to misunderstanding, and may end with a divorce. Further, if you have 6 & 9 as Moolanka & Bhagyanka or vice-versa, marriage life may run into trouble. ***9-6 combination is a symbol of scandals and controversies***.

Remedies:

Uplift the strength of numbers 1, &

5, in the birth chart.

Number 9 & 9:

A person has to face marriage issues if he has 9 as Moolanka and Bhagyanka. On the other hand marriage between 9 & 9 as Moolanka or Bhagyanka may not survive. It is better to avoid the marriage if not been solemnized yet.

Remedies:

Uplift the strength of the numbers 1,5, & 6 in the birth chart.

Number 4 & 4:

4 is Rahu and is a symbol of discipline and organization. A temporary relationship between two 4 is fine but if it is converted to a permanent relationship like marriage or business partnership it would be a disaster.

Remedies;

Uplift the numbers 1, 5, 6, & 7 for better relationships.

Number 8 & 4:

Both 8 and 4 are slow planets. One is the symbol of discipline and another is justice. Temporary relationships between the two are fine. But if the temporary relationships are converted to permanent relationships in the form of business or marriage, they can't survive. A birth chart with 8 & 4 as Bhagyanka or Moolanka may struggle in conjugal life.

Remedies:

Uplift the following numbers i.e. 5,6,3,7 in your birth chart.

Number 8 & 8:

When 8 & 8 are positioned as Moolanka and Bhagyanka, a permanent relationship like a business partnership or a marriage is a problem. It may face issues in marriage or if married conjugal life may come under stress.

Remedies:

Uplift the following numbers i.e. 5,6,3,7 in your birth chart.

Conclusion:

The numbers in your birth chart offer deep insights into your relationships, highlighting both strengths and challenges. Each combination of Moolanka (birth number) and Bhagyanka (life path number) affects how you connect with others, especially in marriage and long-term partnerships. While some numbers like 6 bring harmony, love, and stability, others—like combinations involving 1 & 8, or 2 & 8—signal potential friction and emotional turbulence. Opposing energies from planetary influences such as the Sun (1) and Saturn (8) or the Moon

(2) and Saturn (8) can create difficulties in sustaining long-term bonds.

The analysis suggests that relationships marked by a certain number of pairings may be more prone to misunderstandings, conflicts, or even breakdowns. However, numerology also provides remedies—such as uplifting the strengths of specific numbers (like 5 and 6)—to harmonize the energies and improve the chances of a successful relationship.

Ultimately, understanding these numerical dynamics empowers you to take proactive steps to enhance your relationships. By following the recommended remedies, you can balance your chart's energies and nurture a more fulfilling and stable personal life.

In the next chapter, we will find remedies to nurture and rectify the defects in relationships.

Chapter-5

Remedies for Weak Relationships.

"Numerology illuminates the past, clarifies the present, and shows the future." – Anonymous

(This reflects numerology's role in providing insights across different phases of life.)

Every problem has remedies. It may be simple or can be a little difficult. In numerology, the remedies are the upliftment of the date of birth. These types of remedies include every number, missing numbers as well as numbers present in the chart. I am going to tell you very simple natural and inexpensive remedies to be incorporated into your daily routine as a habit. Now let us go through the remedies for each number. If you have any relationship issues with anyone, how can you resolve them? You might ask for a middleman, who may be the friend of both. When you are angry with your husband and stop talking for a few hours, how can you communicate with him? You may send the message through your child or anyone who is accepted by both. The same principle is applicable in the case of numbers.

1.

SUN

The Sun is the king of the solar system and the birth chart. If the sun is weak in your birth chart you may not be able to communicate your thoughts, in a clear, smart, and articulated manner. You may lose confidence during any discussions and may be **"speech-impaired**." Choosing a profession may be an issue.

Actionable steps;

- ✓ Rise early before sunrise and expose yourself to sunlight.

- ✓ After you wake up in the morning see yourself in the mirror for about 2 minutes.

- ✓ Touch the feet of your parent in the morning. In their absence, you may salute the photographs of your parents.

- ✓ Have a bath putting rose petals in the water.

- ✓ Safeguard the government property.

✓ Offer water to the sun before 7 AM every day (as soon as possible). You may ask how to offer water to the Sun. Is there any prescribed method?

Yes, there is a prescribed way of offering water. Take a round-necked small copper vessel, tie a red thread around its neck, put red vermilion, sunned rice/ "raw rice" (*akshyat*), and sugar/ jaggery in the water, and offer the sun. After bathing take the vessel up to your neck height and drop the water constantly looking at the sun.

The shadow of the falling water must fall on your body. Take care to collect the offering water in a bucket to water the plant. Care must be taken that the offering water must not drop on your legs.

(If you are governed by 8(Moolanka or Bhagyanka) no steps, be taken to appease Sun)

3.

JUPITER

Jupiter is the Guru or the mentor of

Gods. He is the symbol of knowledge, imagination, and creativity. To appease Jupiter and enhance his strength in your birth chart you need to uplift number 3.

Actionable steps;

> Do saffron tilak on your forehead after a bath every day. Do it at the back side of your tongue, and naval point also.

> Every Thursday, water the banana plant and offer jaggery and gram dal. Never forget to offer a ghee lamp to the plant. Remember that the worship of the banana plant should not be made on your own campus. It should be at any public place like a park or temple.

> **(If you are governed by 6(Moolanka or Bhagyanka) no steps, be taken to appease Jupiter)**

4.

RAHU

Rahu is a symbol of discipline and organization. No one can do well in life without discipline in self, workspace, society, etc. Similarly, acting in an organized way for a better cause is beneficial for society. Appease Rahu is necessary for self-discipline and organization.

Actionable steps;

Feed dogs or crows pieces of bread soaked with milk. It may be better to feed them daily. If not possible, do it once or twice a week outside your campus.

5.

MERCURY

Mercury creates balance in life. It is also a symbol of finance and success. Do you remember its place in the Lo-Shu Grid? It is positioned at the center of the chart with an equal distance from every number. To achieve continuous success in personal and professional life, upliftment of number 5 is necessary.

Actionable steps;

> ➢ Free the parrot (green-colored bird) from the cage. On Wednesday buy a parrot, take it home, serve the bird for two to three days, and free it opening the cage. You can do this practice once in three months.

> Use more and more green colors in your life. For example, wear green clothes, use green color pens, and handkerchiefs, eat green vegetables, walk in the park, and enjoy nature under green trees.

6.

VENUS

Venus is a symbol of relationships, family bonding, luxury, and happiness. Imagine a family without love and affection. No good relationships between a couple, and their children. No peace in the family but chaos. The very family structure is disturbed. The absence, or a weak Venus can do all the above issues making life difficult.

Actionable steps;

Donate white things like milk, sugar, barfi, *rasgulla,* etc. to physically challenged persons on Friday. If such persons are not available you may give such things to beggars. Because Venus is considered disabled and has lost one eye during Vaman incarnation of lord Vishnu.

(If you are governed by 3(Moolanka or Bhagyanka) no steps, be taken to appease Venus)

7.

KETU

Ketu is lower part of Rahu. Number 7 is a symbol of wisdom, education, spiritualism, music, dance, drama, and creative awareness.

Actionable steps;

As prescribed for number 4. Feed dogs or crows pieces of bread soaked with milk. It may be better to feed them daily. If not possible, do it once or twice a week outside your campus.

These remedies are simple and can be practiced in your daily schedule. If you need remedies for all your issues then you can read my 2nd book of this series, ***"Numerology: A Practical Guide."***

Conclusion:

Numerology offers simple, practical remedies to address relationship issues and harmonize the energies in your life. By uplifting the numbers in your birth chart, you can bring balance and strength to weak relationships. Each number represents a specific planet and carries unique energies—such as confidence, discipline, communication, and love—necessary for maintaining healthy bonds. For example, appeasing the Sun (1) boosts confidence and clarity in communication, while working with Venus (6) strengthens love and family ties.

The remedies suggested are easy to incorporate into your daily routine, from offering water to the Sun to feeding animals like dogs or crows or freeing a parrot to symbolize balance and freedom. These actions are designed to improve the energies in your life and resolve challenges caused by weak planetary influences.

Ultimately, numerology not only illuminates relationship issues but provides a pathway for healing. Through these simple yet effective remedies, you can align the energies in your chart, nurture healthier relationships, and enjoy a more harmonious personal life. The author's second book, Numerology: A Practical Guide has all the remedies for your upliftment, strength, and growth.

Chapter 6

Love or Arranged Marriage

"Everything is energy and that's all there is to it. Match the frequency of the reality you want."– Albert Einstein

(This aligns with numerology's view that numbers carry specific vibrations and energies that influence our lives.)

In Indian society, marriage is considered a sacrament. Across the different belief systems of human existence, three important ceremonies are observed i.e. the birth rituals, marriage ceremonies, and death rituals. When family and friends observe the birth rituals of a newborn, he can't enjoy or understand them. Similarly, the death rituals left the family and friends to mourn and memories his contributions to his family and society without his physical presence.

Now the only ceremony left for the person to enjoy and cherish is marriage. In Indian society when we think about the marriage of a son or daughter it always reminds us of the arranged marriage with the consent of both the families of bride and groom. Over time, the concept of marriage is changing, and the concept of love marriage is gaining ground in our society. However, marriage is taken very seriously as it is associated with the value system, morality, and cultural backing of society. **Not only in India but in other cultures and civilizations marriage is also taken seriously.**

Do you think numerology or astrology has some clue to conclude which kind of marriage is possible for the person? If you believe in the presence of planets in our universe and they influence our understanding and thinking process, then it is a fact that we can forecast the type of marriage for a person without any doubt. Because everything is connected to a single energy source, that governs the entire universe.

In numerology 5,6 & 7 numbers play a crucial role in a marriage. From the birth chart, we can detect an arranged or love marriage and its stability.

Love Marriage

Example of first scenario,

		2
	5	77

	1	6

M-1 B-6

Second scenario

4		2
	5	777
	1	

M-5, B-7

See the above two birth charts carefully. Our observations are as follows;

- Love marriage is possible with its stability, as 77 and 6 are present. (first scenario)

- When only 77 are present and 6 are absent, a love marriage will happen without stability.

- When 77 and 5 are present a love marriage will happen with a 50% chance of survival.

- If 777 is present love marriage is possible but without the presence of 5 or 6 the marriage mayn't survive.

As you know 5 makes balance in life and has no nonfriends in the chart and 6 represents family, glamor, party, enjoyment, sexual pleasure, etc. 7 is wisdom and it thinks from the heart not from the brain. Ketu can be exploited emotionally so it can go for love and marriage without future planning or consequences. The presence of 6 can guide 7 as 7 is the disciple of 6 (Venus).

Arranged marriage

Example of a scenario;

	9	22
33		
		6

M-3 B-3

In the above chart, there is no chance of a love marriage but an arranged marriage is possible. Why such a prediction? You can ask further. Because,

- Presence of 3(Jupiter) and 9(mars) in the chart are against love marriage.

- Multiple 3 and 6 present calls for an arranged marriage.

- If MOOLANKA-BHAGYANKA are 2,3,9 symbolizes arranged marriage.

However, the past life experiences of different incarnations and karmic accounts make a difference in shaping people's lives.

Conclusion:

When it comes to the question of love marriage versus arranged marriage, the perspective is deeply rooted in individual and cultural values. In Indian society, both types of marriages are seen as significant, each with its own set of traditions and expectations.

Numerology offers an intriguing lens through which we can see these marital paths. By analyzing numbers in your birth chart, we can gain insights into the likelihood of a love marriage or an arranged one, and how stable that marriage might be.

For those who find 5, 6, and 7 prominently featured in their charts, love marriages often appear as a viable and potentially stable option. However, the presence of these numbers alone doesn't guarantee success. Your mindset and family influences can also play crucial roles.

On the other hand, a chart dominated by 3, 9, and multiple instances of 3 suggests that arranged marriages are more likely. These numbers align more closely with traditional values and stability in marital status.

Ultimately, while numerology can provide guidance, the choice between love and arranged marriage is deeply personal. It is further influenced by many factors, including past experiences and individual preferences. Whether you are drawn to the romance of a love marriage or the stability of an arranged one, what matters most is the mutual respect, understanding, and commitment you bring to the relationship.

Chapter 7

Your Health is Wealth

Life is the flower for which love is the honey. But the fragrance comes from the numbers that surround us." – Victor Hugo

(Although metaphorical, this quote suggests that numbers shape the structure and harmony of life.)

"Your health is your greatest wealth. Take care of it." - Unknown

Your health is your big wealth.

"Your health is your greatest wealth. Take care of it." - Unknown

No one wants it to be stolen. If your health is weakening it justifies that you are losing your money and peace of mind. Further, the pain experienced due to harm to your tissues, bone, skin, or organs is to be born alone. Money for the treatment may be collected or arranged from different sources but you have to suffer from the pain. Nobody can share it only can console and stand by your side.

Some belief systems say that the disease we experience, the debt we owe, and the enemies we face are the balance of our karmic accounts.

"The past is never dead. It's not even past."
- William Faulkner

Our sufferings or happiness are the compound effects of our actions for different birth and rebirth. We can detect your health sector from your birth chart.

Detection of Weak Health from your Birth Chart.

Some *Moolanka* and *Bhagyanka* combinations can help us to detect your health sector.

M	B
2	8
3	6
4	9
6	3
8	2
9	4

2 & 8 Combination:

This is an anti-combination. The above combinations of **Moolanka -Bhagyanka** or vice-versa reflect the weak health sector. Why such a situation? Remember 2 is the moon and 8 is Saturn. Water symbolizes the moon, whereas iron is the symbol of Saturn. What would happen, if both the elements were kept together? The iron will start decaying coming in contact with the water. Decaying means the weakening of your body by the disease. For this happening you are not solely responsible in this life but rather accrued for several births and rebirth. But you have to be cautious about your health.

The health issues may be related to poor blood circulation, nervousness, and mental stress.

3 & 6 combinations:

3 represents Jupiter and 6 is Venus. This is an anti-combination, as they don't like to see each other's face or company. Why such an attitude? Both represent two different ideologies, civilizations, and mindsets. Jupiter is the master/guru of Dev/gods whereas Venus is the master of devils. Both are the powerhouse of knowledge, but they can't tolerate each other due to their commitments to their own culture. Now think of two crocodiles of different breeds put in a tank and its bitter results. It will make the water muddy and engage in fighting. The antiplanet does the same thing. They destroy your health ecosystem and make you diseased.

4 & 9 combinations:

4 is Rahu and 9 is Mars. Rahu is without body and heart. He thinks from his brain. He is a gangster and loves to enjoy wine and tamasic nature. However, Mars is a commander and fighter. His nature is sattvic and disciplined. They can stay together for some time but not for a long time. Mars never allows non-sattvic activities of Rahu. Staying together means conflicts in the health ecosystem leading to bloodshed. **This opposite combination is responsible for surgery.**

DETECTION OF HEALTH ISSUES FROM MOOLANKA

MOOLANKA

1.

The people born on any of the following dates of 1, 10,19, or 28 of any month governed by Moolanka 1.

People may experience heart-related diseases, high blood pressure, eye problems, and throat issues.

2.

The people born on 2, 11, or 20 of any month are governed by the number 2.

They may experience stomach issues, reproductive problems, poor blood circulation, sleeplessness, and mental stress.

3.

The people born on 3, 12, 21, or 30 are treated as governed by Moolanka 3.

These types of people may suffer from diabetics, hips or thigh trouble, joint pain, liver or lung issues.

4.

The date of birth falls on 4, 13, 22, or 31 are governed by number 4.

The people who have 4 as Moolanka may face an accident, undergo critical surgery, ankle and strength-related issues, muscle tension, kidney and urinary tract infections, and addiction.

5.

We can get 5 from the date of birth, 5, 14, or 23.

The people of Moolanka 5 may experience pain in their hands, nervous system, and sleep disorders.

6.

The date of birth 6, 15, and 24 are coming under Moolanka 6.

The people of this Moolanka neglect their own health for others. They may experience throat issues, and lung, heart, or lower back problems.

7.

The people born on 7, 16, or 25 are governed by Moolanka 7.

They may feel nervous system-related issues, eye problems, nasal congestion, etc.

8.

We get Moolanka from the date of birth, 8, 17, and 26. They are normally blessed with good health. However, they may experience issues like constipation and lower back problems.

9.

The people born on 9, 18, or 27 are governed by Moolanka 9.

These types of people may face shoulder, head, and heart-related issues. They are prone to accidents, and stitches at their bodies at least once in their lifetime.

If the planets are weak, they can give unfavorable results in the form of health, relationships, and employment issues.

Remedies for Weak Health

We are part and parcel of the different elements and their imbalance creates different issues including health problems for us, we can also use them for our betterment. The different elements can be used to redress the absence of missing numbers and upliftment of Moolanka and Bhagyanka.

DIFFERENT NUMBERS REPRESENT DIFFERENT ELEMENTS.

4 WOOD	9 FIRE	2 EARTH
3 WOOD	5 EARTH	7 METAL SILVER
8 EARTH	1 WATER	6 METAL GOLDEN

Lo-Shu Grid

1→Water Element

2→ Earth Element

3→ Wood Element

4→Wood Element.

5→Earth Element.

6→Golden Metal

7→ Silver Metal

8→ Earth Element.

9→ Fire Element.

Wood Elements:

As 3 & 4 represent wood elements, we compensate for their absence from the birth chart with the use of wood elements.

Rudrakshya (seeds of the Elaeocarpus ganitrus tree), Tulsi (Basil), Chandal(sandalwood), or any type of wood.

- Wear any rudrakshya (five-faced) mala, tulsi bead mala, or sandal mala around your neck. For spiritual sanctity, the mala should consist of 108 beads.

- You may also wear a wooden bracelet around your wrist.

Earth Elements:

2,5 & 8 form the diagonal line in the Lo-Shu grid were called the earth element. Using the earth elements, we may compensate for their absence from our birth chart and enhance their power.

Crystal is considered an earth element.

- Wear **a** crystal bracelet around your left wrist.

- You may also wear a crystal mala around your neck.

- You may also wear crystal even if with the presence of 2,5 and 8 numbers.

- Crystal can help you make clear decisions. Further, it can help, you include healing, meditation, and enhancing specific qualities or energies.

Fire Elements:

9 is a fire element. Fire means energy.

Red threads and red clothes can be used as fire elements.

- Wear red thread around your right wrist (in the case of male) and around your left arm (in case of female).

- Wear red clothes, and keep a red handkerchief with you. Clean the threads regularly.

Water Element:

1 is a water element.

- Drink sufficient water. If you drink 2 liters of water daily, increase it to 2.5 to 3 liters.

- Offer water to the sun daily preferably before 7 AM.

- After a bath take the copper vessel up to your neck height and drop the water constantly looking at the sun. The shadow of the falling water must fall on your body.

- Take care to collect the offering water in a bucket to water the plant.

Silver Metal

Number 7 represents silver metal.

- Wear a metal strap wristwatch of golden and silver mixed color.

Golden Metal:

Number 6 represents the golden metal. But remember 6 represents white color.

- Wear a metal strap wristwatch of golden color. The dial of the watch must be reasonably bigger with the 1 to 12 marking.

- The number indicating 6 must be visible clearly without any cut.

These are very simple and inexpensive methods that can enhance your confidence and improve your health. Have faith in yourself and your belief system.

SPECIAL AND IMPORTANT HEALTH REMEDIES:

Chanting of Gayatri Mantra:

If anyone is suffering from a serious illness and after proper medication, his health is not recovering as expected, then he has to recite the **Gayatri mantra** as many times as possible with utmost faith. ***In the case of infants, his/her parents can recite the Gayatri mantra at least 108 times every day.***

Gayatri Mantra

ॐ भूर्भुवः स्वः।

तत्सवितुर्वरेण्यं।

भर्गो देवस्य धीमहि।

धियो यो नः प्रचोदयात्॥

Om Bhūr bhuvaḥ svaḥ |

Tat savitur vareṇyaṁ |

Bhargo devasya dhīmahi |

Dhiyo yo naḥ pracodayāt ||

<u>Wear Gayatri Yantra</u>

One can wear *Gayatri Yantra* to get rid of complicated health issues. Everyone can wear this Yantra on Sunday.

Conclusion:

In this comprehensive exploration of numerology and health, it becomes evident that our Moolanka (birth number) and Bhagyanka (life path number) can significantly influence our physical well-being. The combinations of certain numbers, such as 2 and 8, or 3 and 6, reveal potential health challenges linked to imbalances in planetary energies. By understanding these number combinations and their elemental associations, we can proactively address health concerns. Remedies involving wood, earth, fire, water, and metal elements—along with spiritual practices like the Gayatri Mantra—offer a holistic approach to improving health and maintaining balance in life.

Conclusion

Numerology is not just a study of numbers— it's a pathway to understanding the hidden power of life. Your date of birth holds hidden information that needs to be decoded. A properly decoded date of birth can reveal your strengths, weaknesses, and life's direction. By applying the principles of numerology, you can unlock new perspectives on your career, relationships, health, and future. It's not about superstition; it's about harnessing the power of ancient knowledge to improve your life and the lives of those around you.

As we have experienced numbers are everywhere and integral to our existence from birth to death. They are also the foundation of the universe, and by understanding their influence, you can do better planning for your personal journey.

Whether you believe in numerology as a science or view it as ancient wisdom its impact is undeniable and beyond debate. Its wise applications in life can make you from weak to strong, powerless to powerful. As you continue on this path of discovery, remember that numerology offers not just predictions, but practical tools for self-improvement and growth.

Every problem has solutions. Never be disappointed in your life. Life is not a bed of roses but of challenges. Face the challenges with the solutions of numerology and unlock your true potential.

In numerology, each number holds its own unique characteristics, much like individuals possess distinct traits. Starting from numbers 1 to 9 aligned with planets shaping personality, behavior, and life outcomes. For instance, the leadership and resilience of Moolanka 1 reflect the influence of the Sun, while the emotional sensitivity and diplomacy of Moolanka 2 mirror the qualities of the Moon.

As we move through the numbers, we see different attributes emerge—Jupiter's wisdom in Moolanka 3, Rahu's rebellious nature in Moolanka 4, Mercury's balance in Moolanka 5, and so on. Each number brings both strengths and challenges, reminding us that every individual is a blend of qualities, much like the numbers themselves.

The fascinating part of numerology is understanding the characteristics of anti and opposite numbers. For example, the friction between Moolanka 1 and 8 reflects the ancient story of the Sun and Saturn, where the differences are deeply rooted yet irreconcilable.

Ultimately, numerology provides a powerful tool to comprehend human nature, and at the same time offers insight into our strengths, weaknesses, and potential paths. It guides us to understand ourselves better and the world around us.

Now you understand the characteristics of the numbers. In the next chapter, we see how the numbers (Moolanka & Bhagyanka) behave with each other.

With the compatibility of numbers, we see how each number vibrates at its own frequency, creating relationships that mirror real-life dynamics. The concept of compatibility is beautifully illustrated through the lens of friendship, neutrality, and enmity, with each number representing a celestial or mythological entity. For example, the Sun (1) and Saturn (8) clash like fire and iron, while the Sun's strong bond with Mars (9) signifies the unbreakable connection between a king and his commander. These patterns give us insight into how numbers influence our relationships, both personal and professional.

Ultimately, understanding the compatibility of numbers allows us to understand better our interactions and make informed decisions. Whether building friendships, partnerships, or alliances, knowing the rhythm of these numbers can guide us toward harmonious outcomes or help us avoid potential conflicts.

As we continue, and learn more about this fascinating subject, we'll uncover deeper layers of meaning and practical applications that help align our lives with the cosmic rhythm around us.

The numbers in your birth chart offer deep insights into your relationships, highlighting both strengths and challenges. Each combination of Moolanka (birth number) and Bhagyanka (life path number) affects how you connect with others, especially in marriage and long-term partnerships. While some numbers like 6 bring harmony, love, and stability, others—like combinations involving 1 & 8, or 2 & 8—signal potential friction and emotional turbulence. Opposing energies from planetary influences such as the Sun (1) and Saturn (8) or the Moon (2) and Saturn (8) can create difficulties in sustaining long-term bonds.

The analysis suggests that relationships marked by a certain number of pairings may be more prone to misunderstandings, conflicts, or even breakdowns. However, numerology also provides remedies—such as uplifting the strengths of specific numbers (like 5 and 6)—to harmonize the energies and improve the chances of a successful relationship.

Ultimately, understanding these numerical dynamics empowers you to take proactive steps to enhance your relationships. By following the recommended remedies, you can balance your chart's energies and nurture a more fulfilling and stable personal life.

Numerology offers simple, practical remedies to address relationship issues and harmonize the energies in your life. By uplifting the numbers in your birth chart, you can bring balance and strength to weak relationships. Each number represents a specific planet and carries unique energies—such as confidence, discipline, communication, and love—necessary for maintaining healthy bonds. For example, appeasing the Sun (1) boosts confidence and clarity in communication, while working with Venus (6) strengthens love and family ties.

The remedies suggested are easy to incorporate into your daily routine, from offering water to the Sun to feeding animals like dogs or crows or freeing a parrot to symbolize balance and freedom. These actions are designed to improve the energies in your life and resolve challenges caused by weak planetary influences.

Ultimately, numerology not only illuminates relationship issues but provides a pathway for healing. Through these simple yet effective remedies, you can align the energies in your chart, nurture healthier relationships, and enjoy a more harmonious personal life. The author's second book, Numerology: A Practical Guide has all the remedies for your upliftment, strength, and growth.

When it comes to the question of love marriage versus arranged marriage, the perspective is deeply rooted in individual and cultural values. In Indian society, both types of marriages are seen as significant, each with its own set of traditions and expectations.

Numerology offers an intriguing lens through which we can see these marital paths. By analyzing numbers in your birth chart, we can gain insights into the likelihood of a love marriage or an arranged one, and how stable that marriage might be.

For those who find 5, 6, and 7 prominently featured in their charts, love marriages often appear as a viable and potentially stable option. However, the presence of these numbers alone doesn't guarantee success. Your mindset and family influences can also play crucial roles.

On the other hand, a chart dominated by 3, 9, and multiple instances of 3 suggests that arranged marriages are more likely. These numbers align more closely with traditional values and stability in marital status.

Ultimately, while numerology can provide guidance, the choice between love and arranged marriage is deeply personal. It is further influenced by many factors, including past experiences and individual preferences. Whether you are drawn to the romance of a love marriage or the stability of an arranged one, what matters most is the mutual respect, understanding, and commitment you bring to the relationship.

In this comprehensive exploration of numerology and health, it becomes evident that our Moolanka (birth number) and Bhagyanka (life path number) can significantly influence our physical well-being. The combinations of certain numbers, such as 2 and 8, or 3 and 6, reveal potential health challenges linked to imbalances in planetary energies. By understanding these number combinations and their elemental associations, we can proactively address health concerns. Remedies involving wood, earth, fire, water, and metal elements—along with spiritual practices like the Gayatri Mantra—offer a holistic approach to improving health and maintaining balance in life.

Life is beautiful, your perceptions matter.

Disclaimer

"Numerology for Health and Relationship", is designed to offer insights based on numerology, which is an ancient system of understanding numbers and their influence on our lives. However, it's important to remember that the content in this book is for informational and educational purposes only.

The advice and remedies suggested are not intended to replace professional guidance from a doctor, therapist, or relationship counselor. If you're dealing with serious health issues or relationship problems, please consult with a qualified healthcare provider or professional expert. Numerology can be a helpful tool for self-reflection and personal growth, but it should be used alongside other trusted forms of support.

Results and interpretations of numerology can vary from person to person. Use the guidance in this book with an open mind and heart, and always make decisions that feel right for you and your unique situation.

May I Ask You for a Small Favor?

At the outset, I want to give a big thanks for taking out time to read this book. You could have chosen any other book, but you chose mine, and I totally appreciate this.

I hope you got at least a few actionable insights that will have a positive impact on your day-to-day life.

Can I ask for 30 seconds more of your time?

I would love it if you could leave a review about the book. Reviews may not matter to big-name authors; but they're a tremendous help for authors like me, who don't have many followers. They help me grow my readership by encouraging folks to take a chance on my books.

To put it straight, reviews are the lifeblood of any author. I feel this book ***Numerology for Health and Relationship** *, shall enrich you with some actionable steps.

Please leave your review by visiting the "**Review Section** "of this book's page on this platform.

It will just take less than a minute of your time, but will tremendously help me to reach out to more people, so please leave your review.

Thanks for your support of my work. And I would love to see your review.